GEOMETRIC DESIGNS
COLORING BOOK

4 BOOKS IN 1!

DELUXE EDITION

DOVER PUBLICATIONS, INC.
MINEOLA, NEW YORK

NOTE

Serious colorists of all ages will enjoy the artistic challenge offered by the geometric figures, fractals, prismatic patterns, and abstract shapes that fill the pages of this book. Unlike coloring books that feature everyday objects, over 100 illustrations offer limitless possibilities for exploring the usage of color. Plus, perforated pages will make displaying your work easy!

Bibliographical Note

Geometric Designs Coloring Book: Deluxe Edition is a new compilation of previously published Dover books by Jeremy Elder, Hop David, Peter Von Thenen, and John Wik. See source information below.

Source Information

Deco Tech Geometric Coloring Book (2010), *GeoScapes* (2013), *Graphic Art Designs* (2013), *Prismatic Designs* (2013).

International Standard Book Number

ISBN-13: 978-0-486-77776-4
ISBN-10: 0-486-77776-6

Manufactured in the United States by Courier Corporation
77776601   2013
www.doverpublications.com

GRAPHIC ART
DESIGNS

JEREMY ELDER

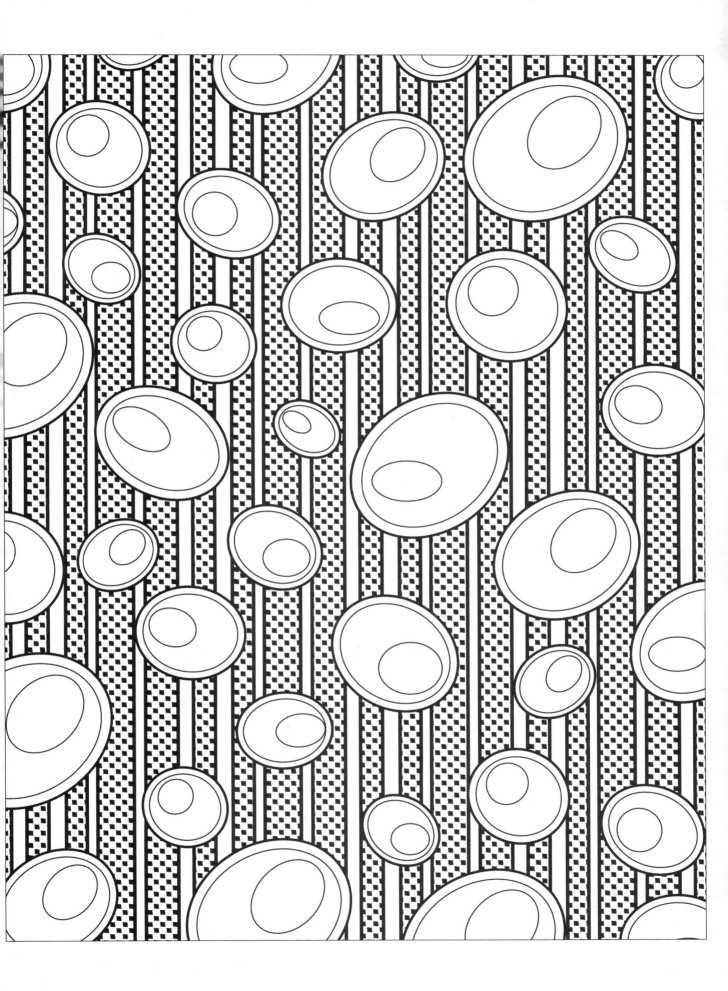

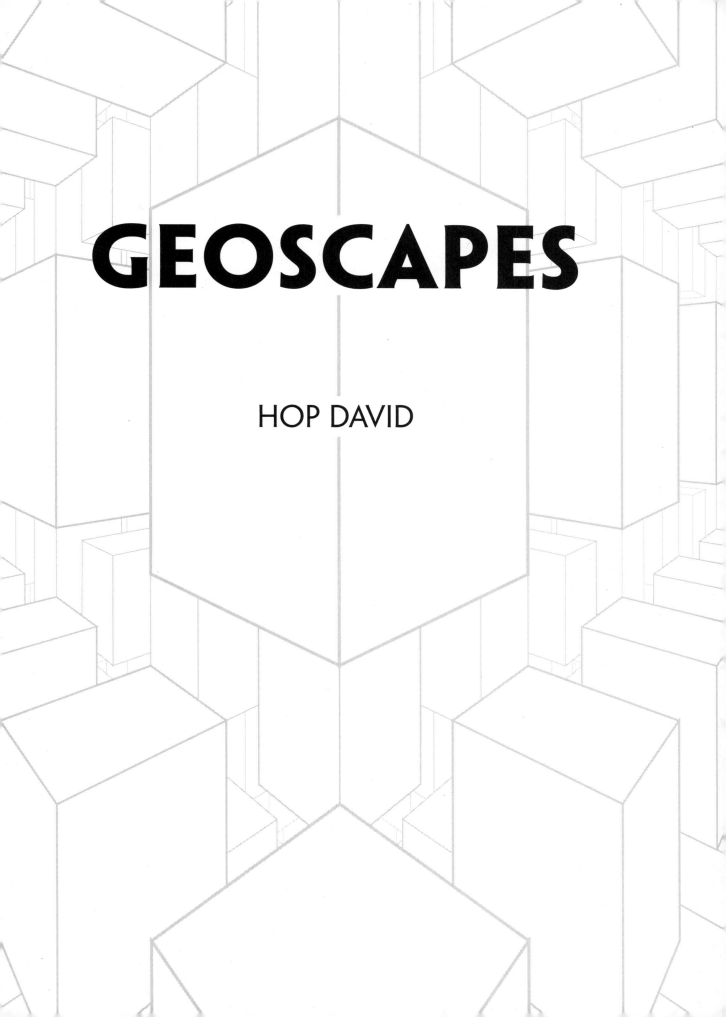

GEOSCAPES

HOP DAVID

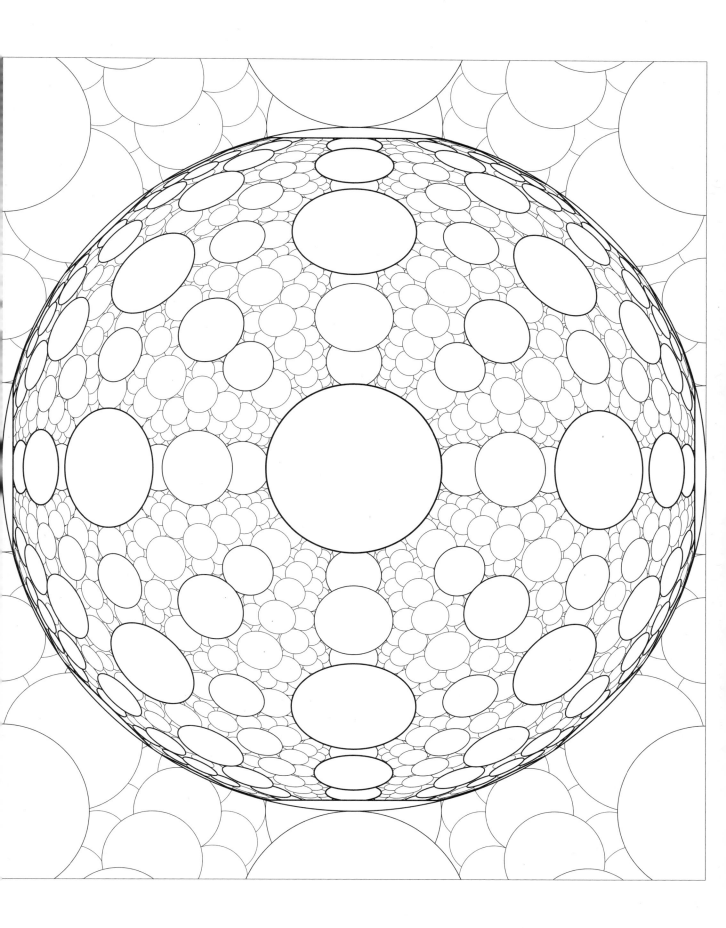

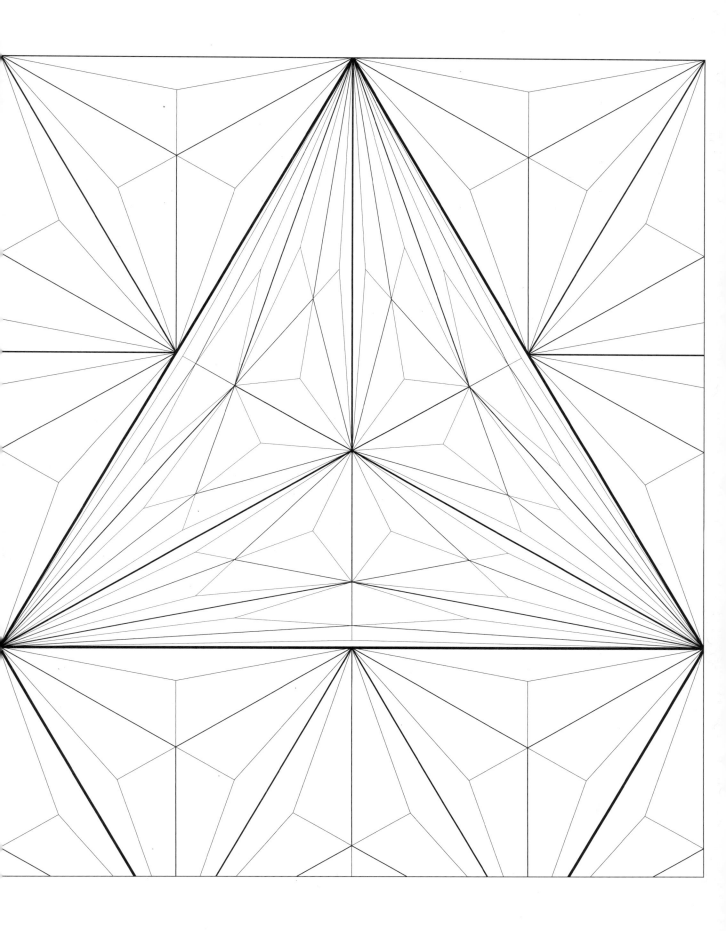

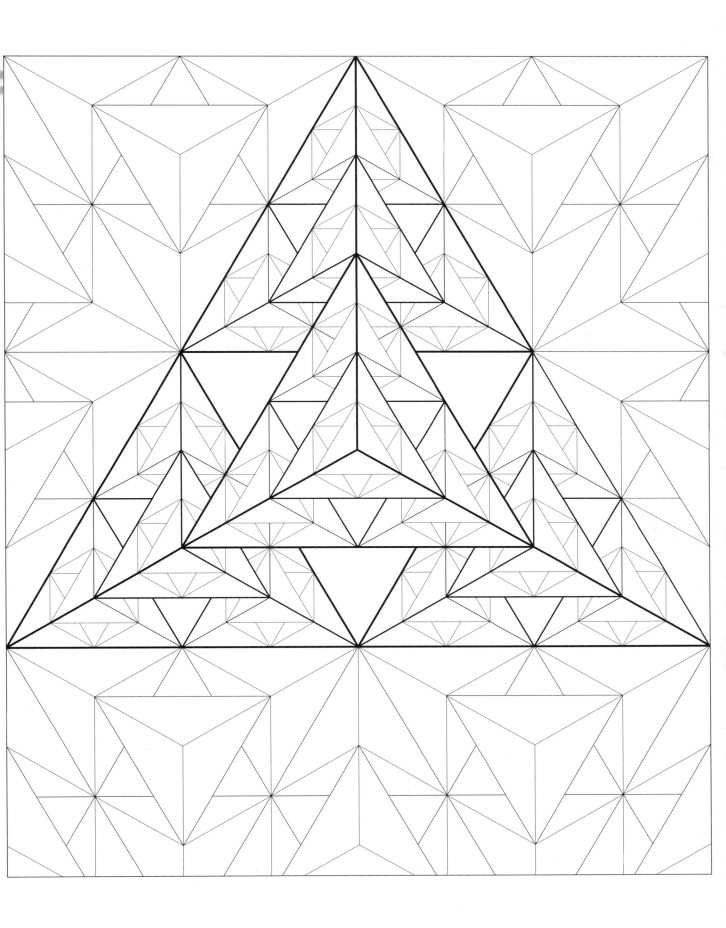

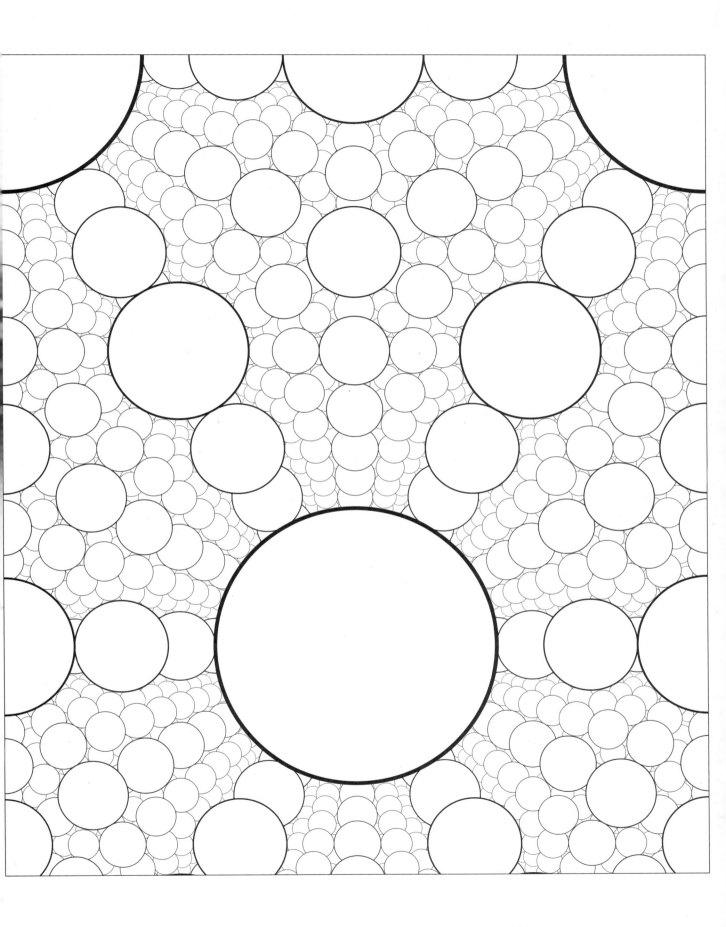

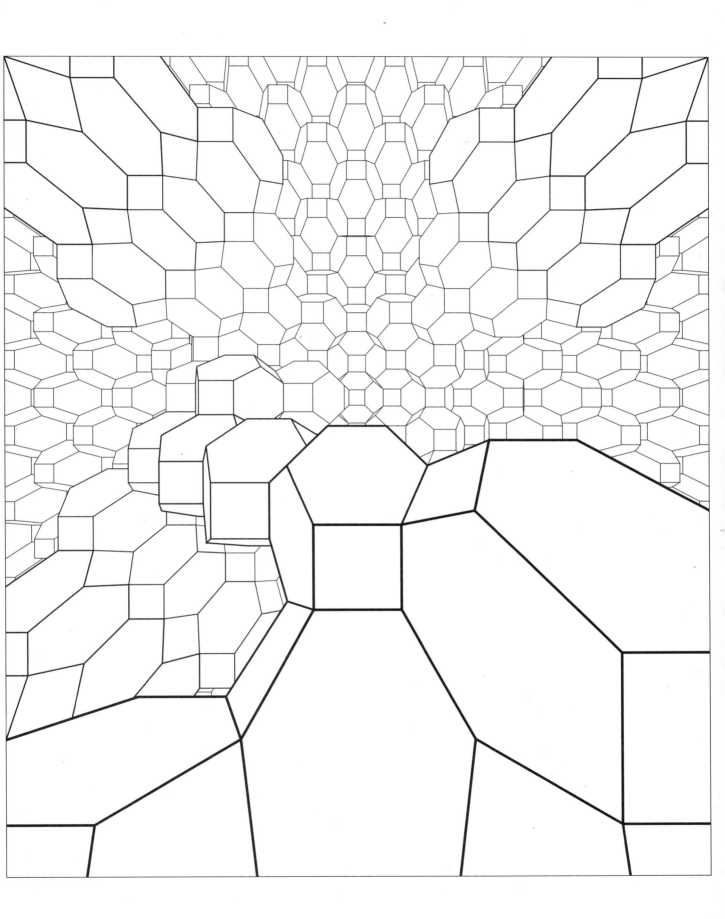

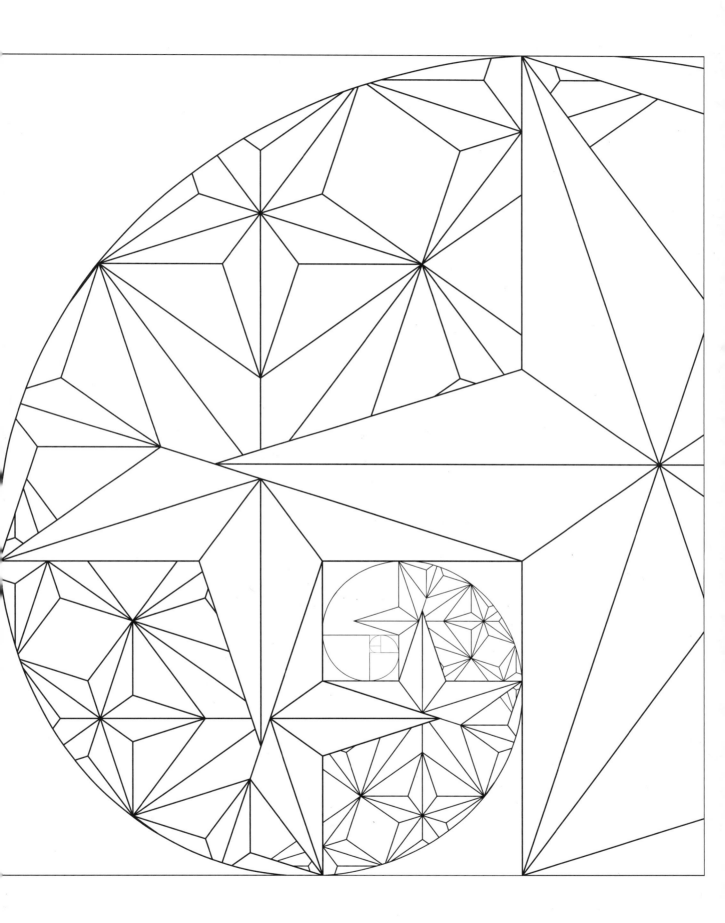

PRISMATIC
DESIGNS

PETER VON THENEN

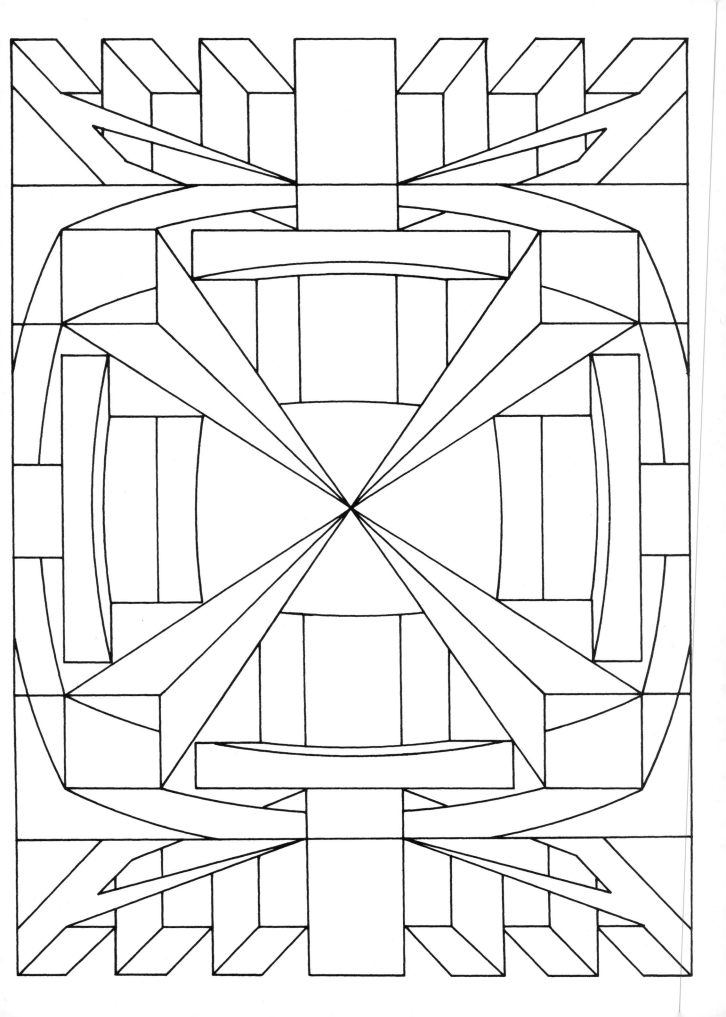

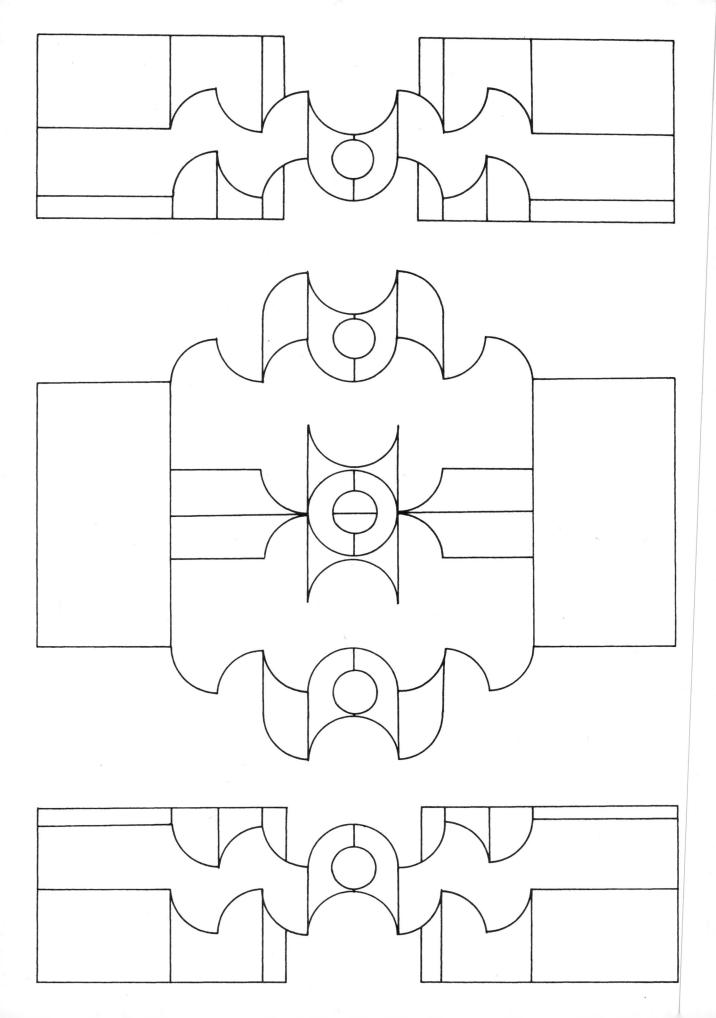

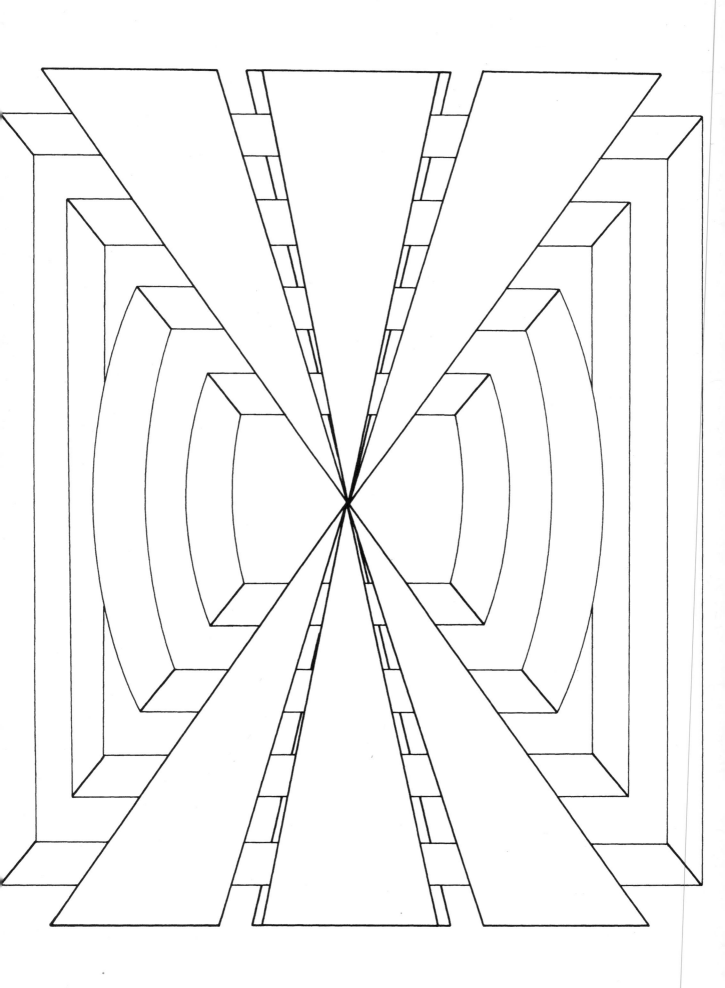

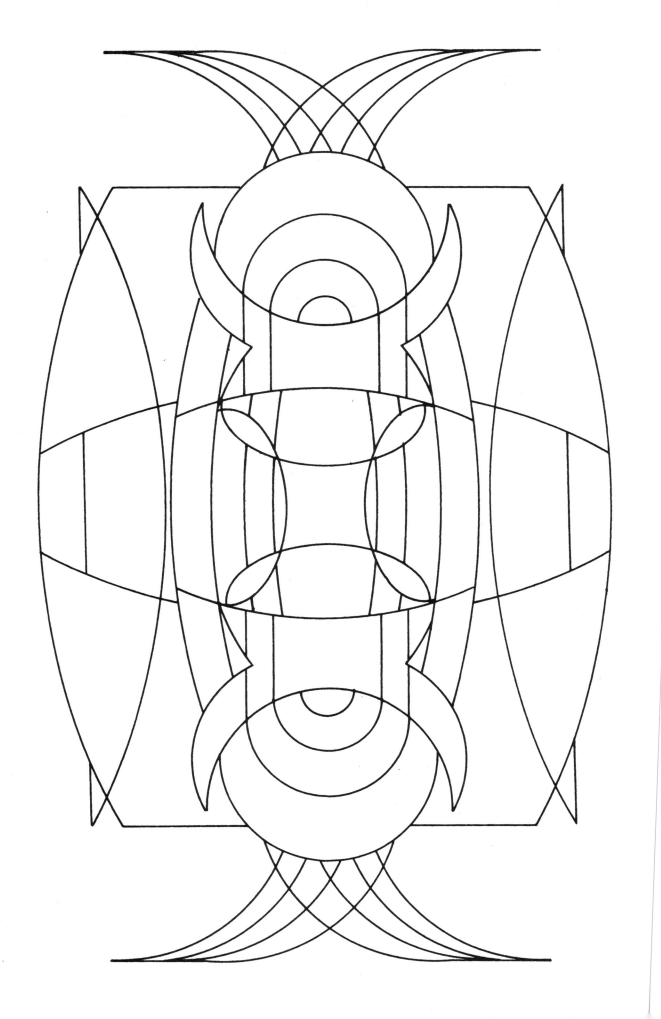

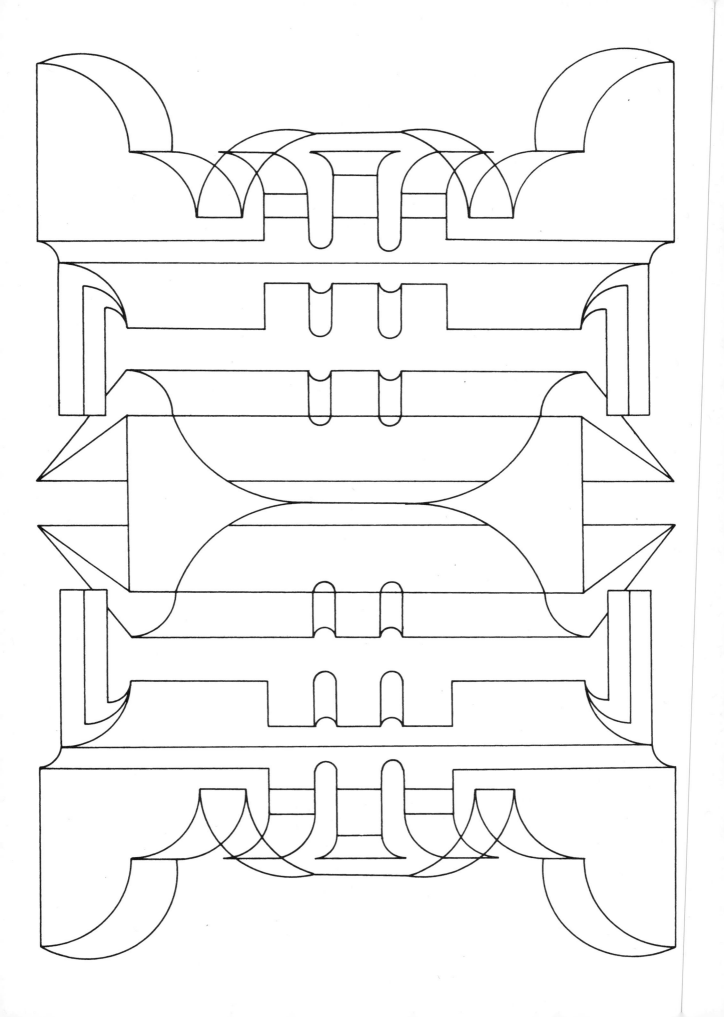

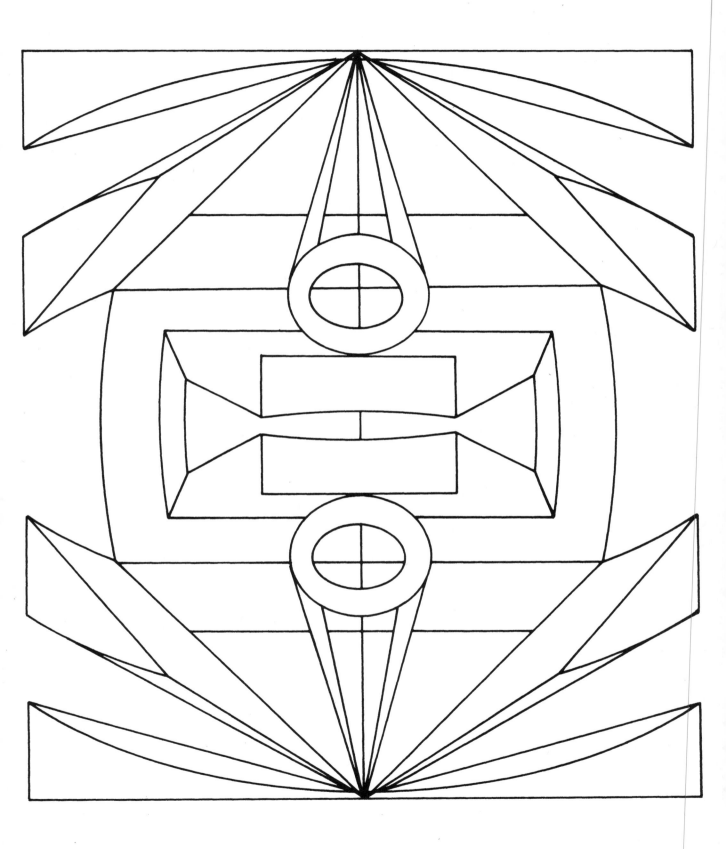

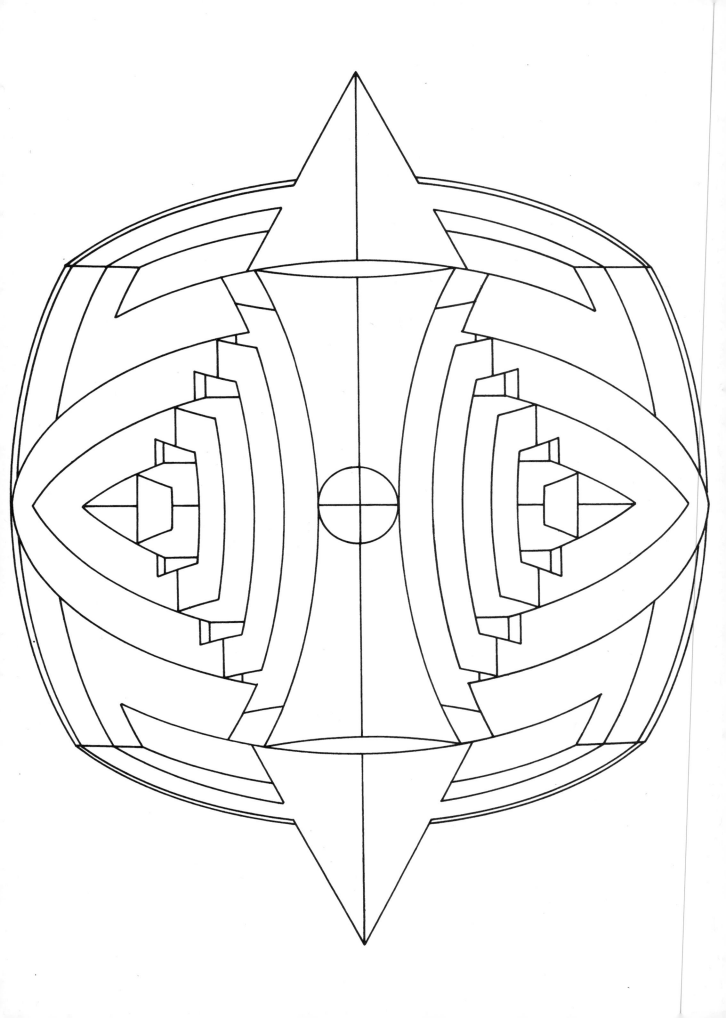

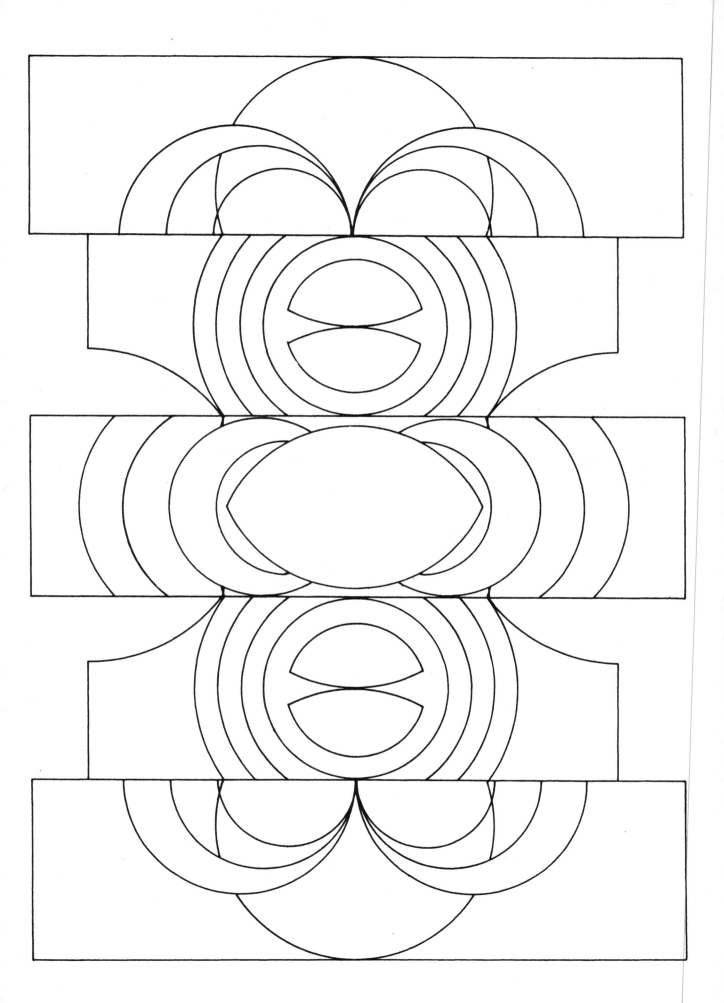

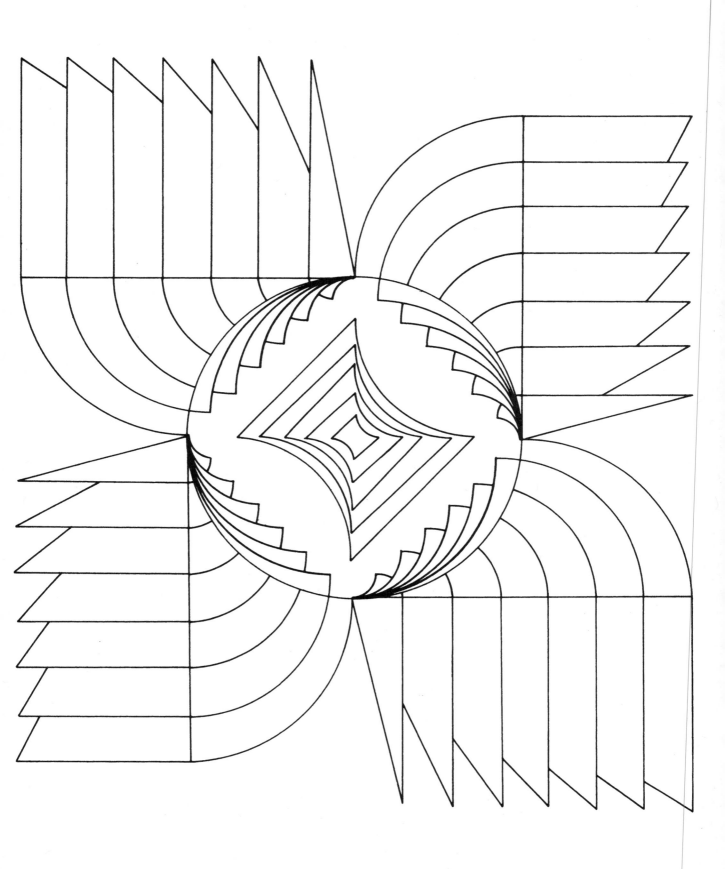

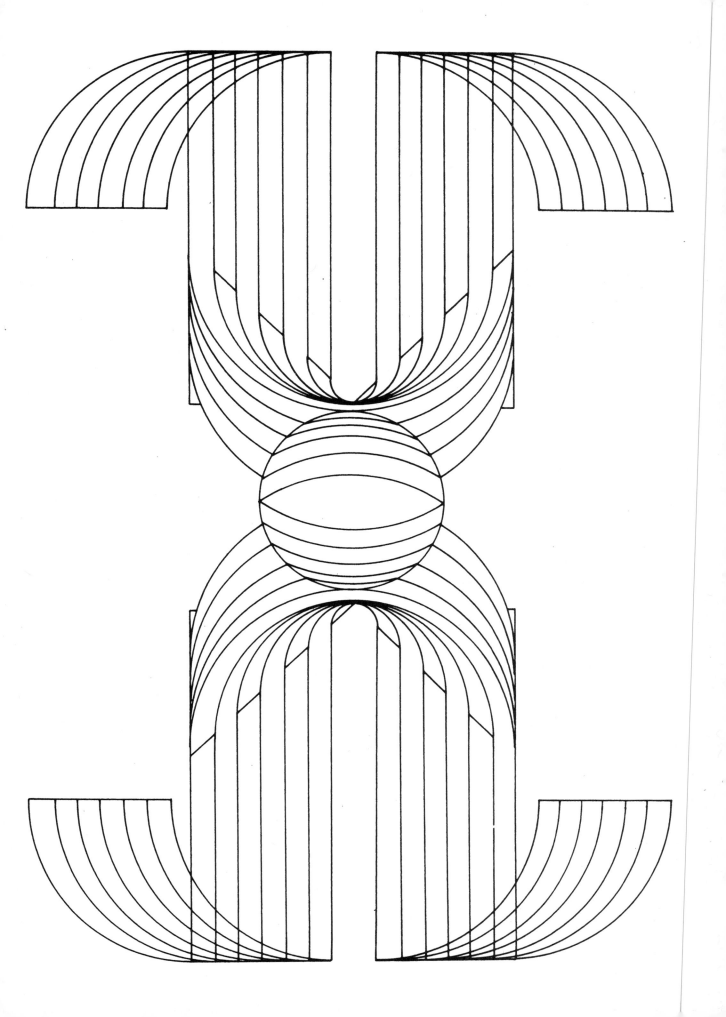

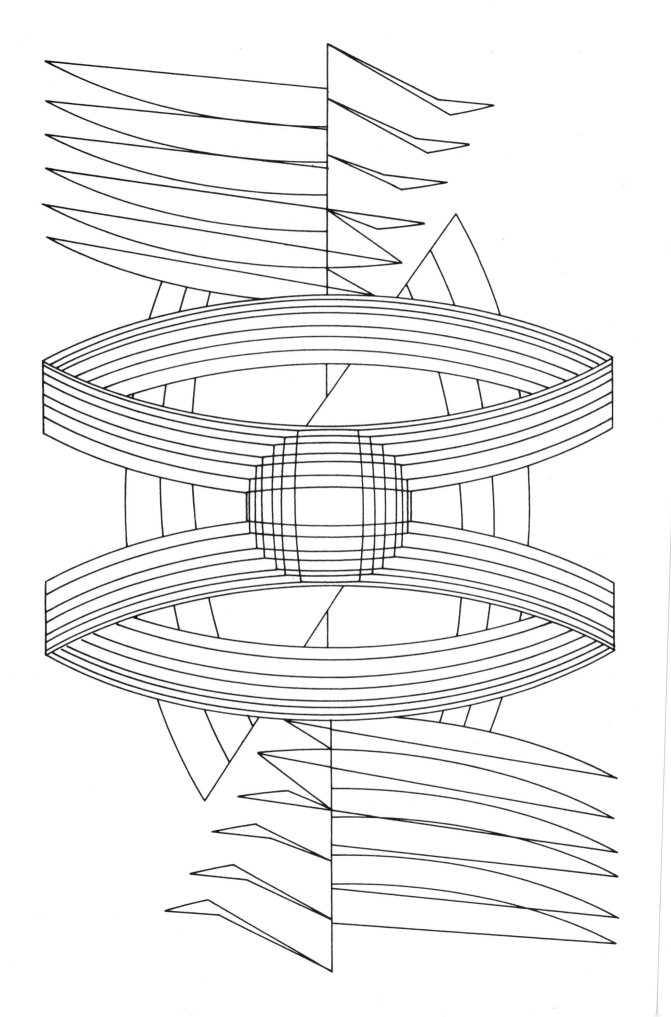

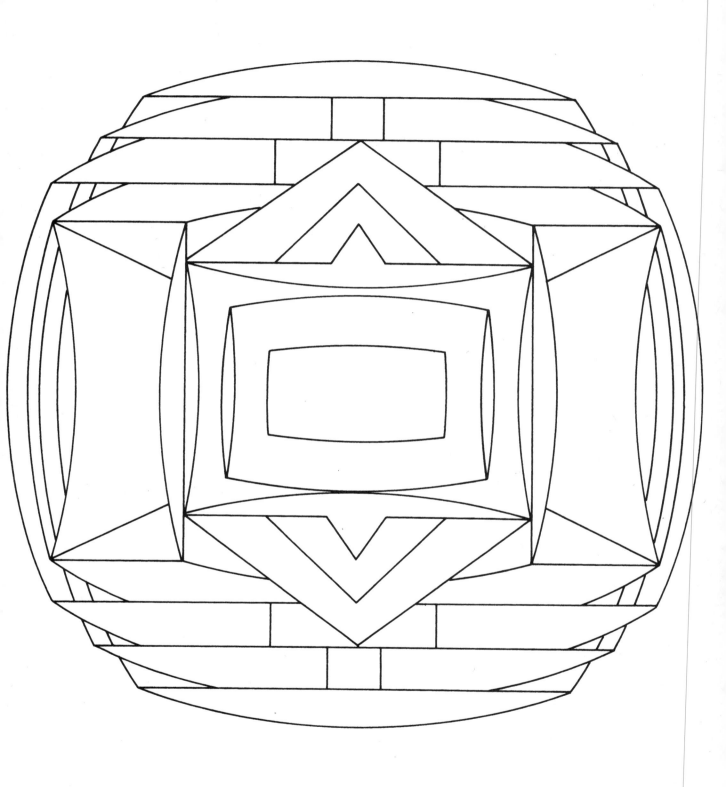

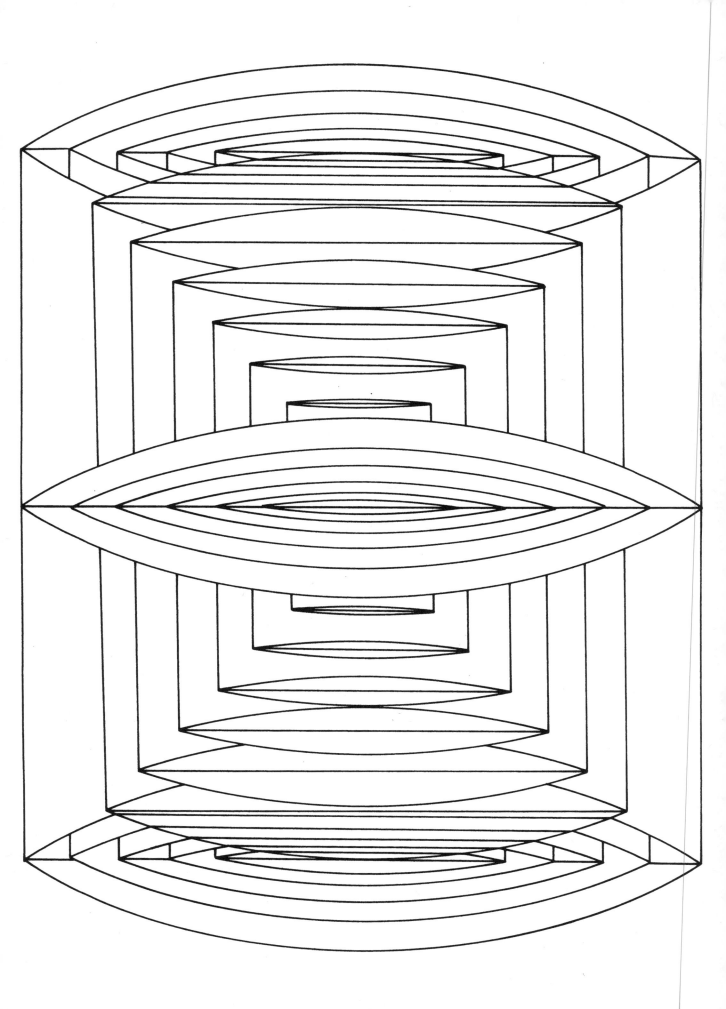

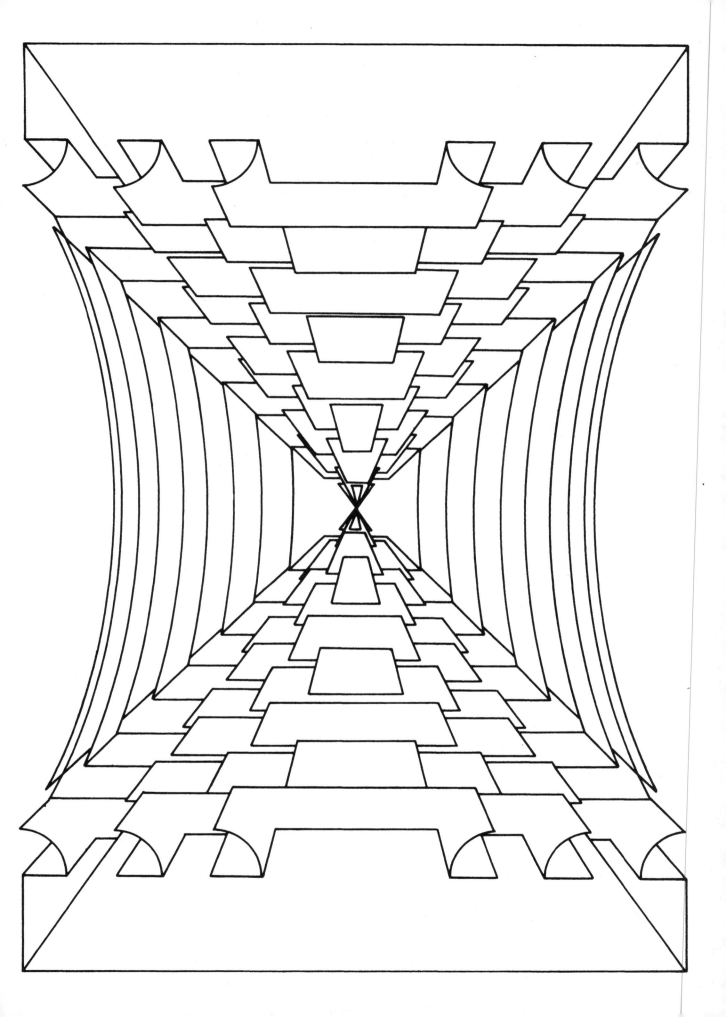

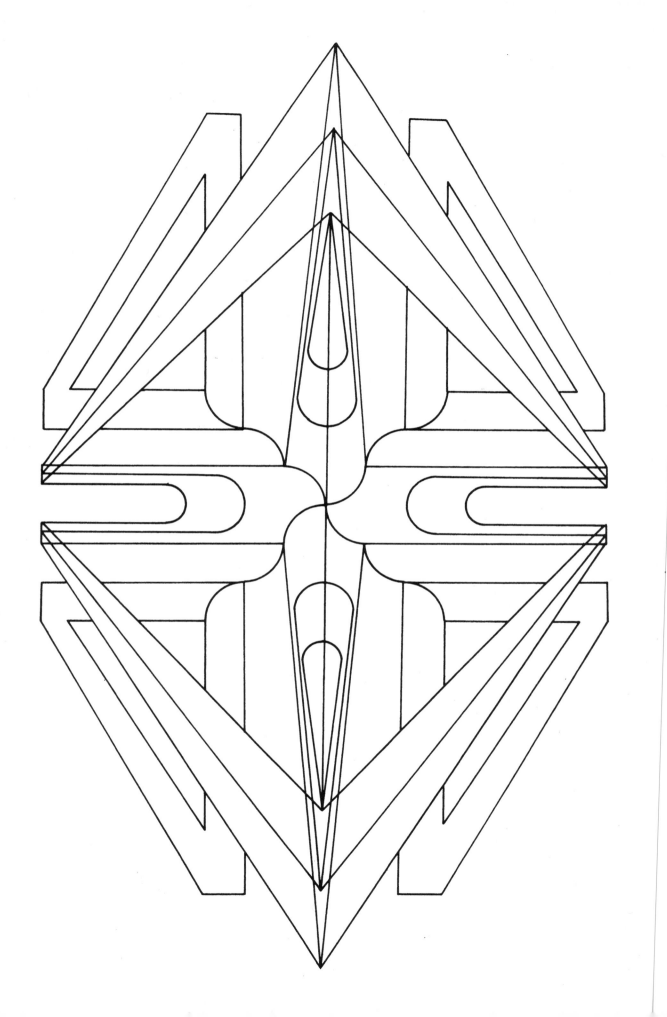

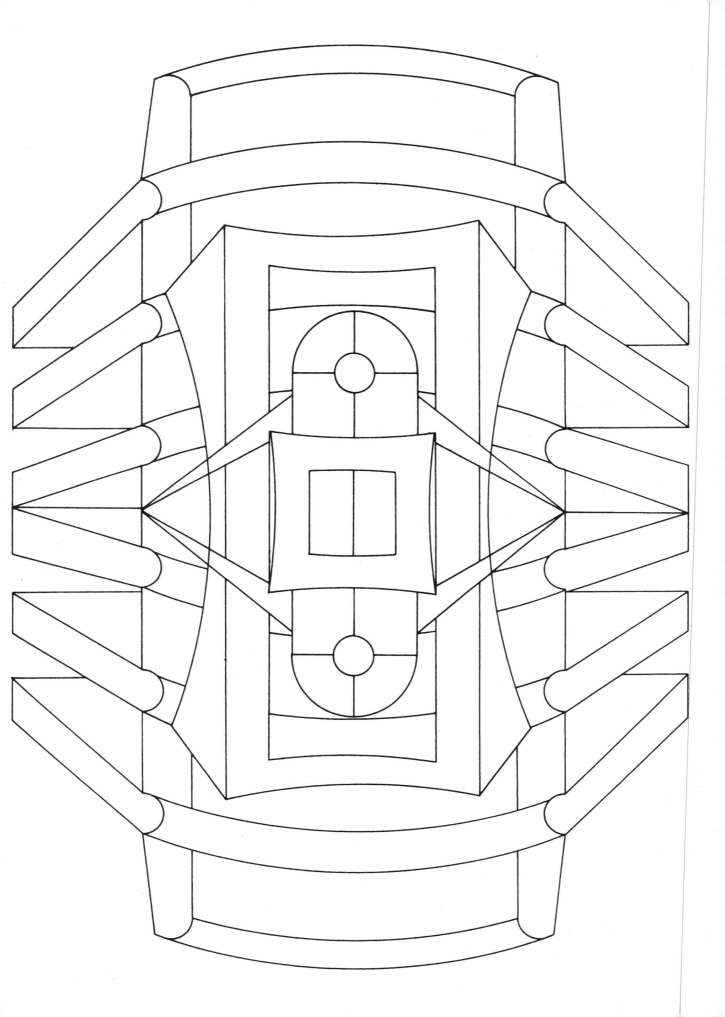

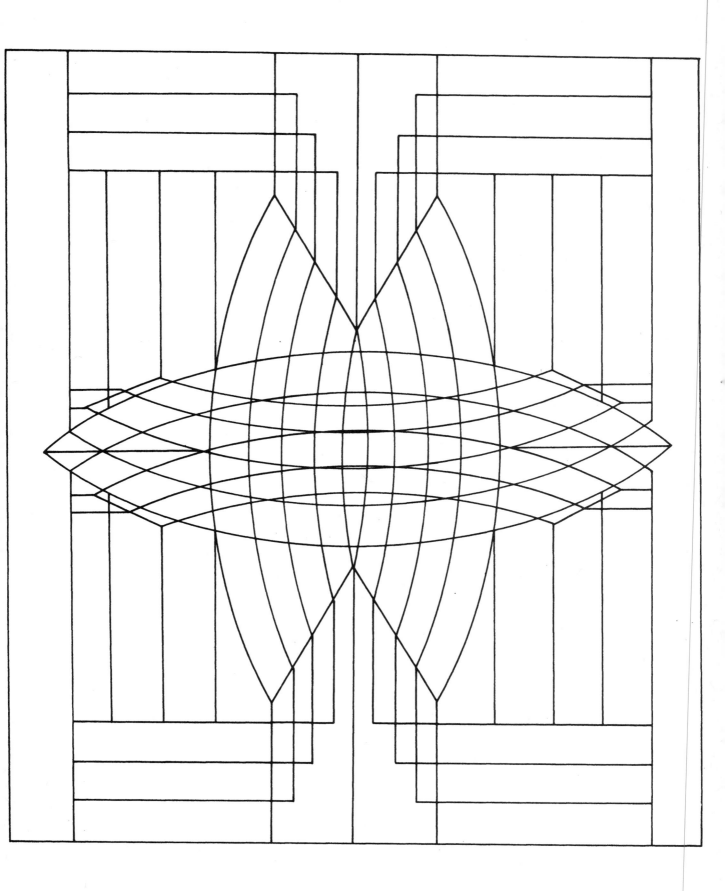

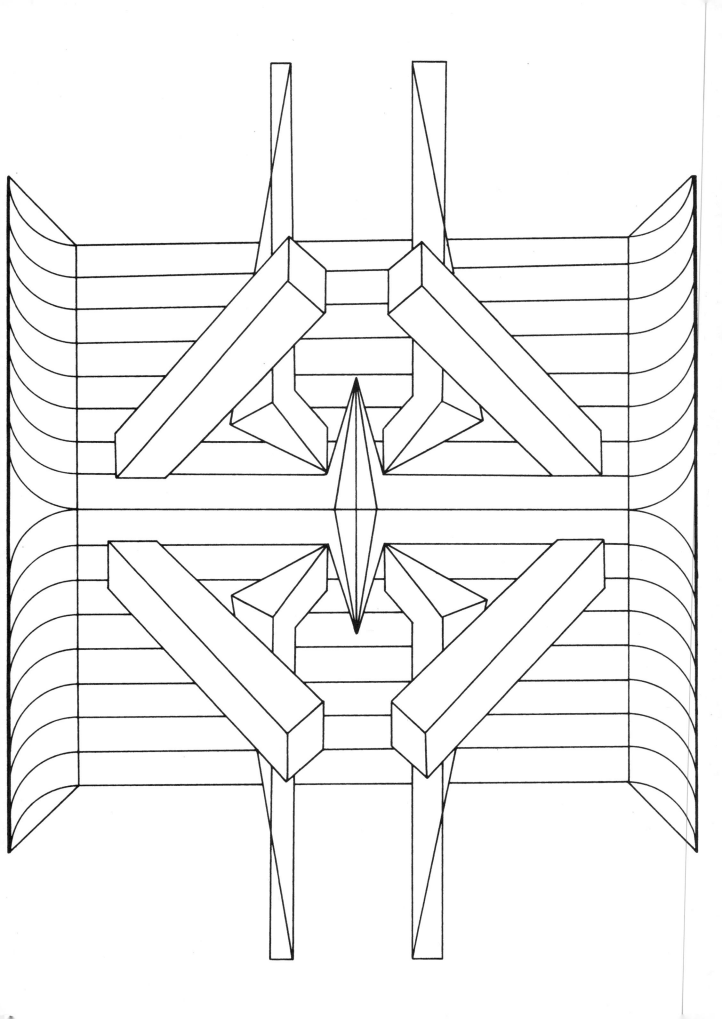

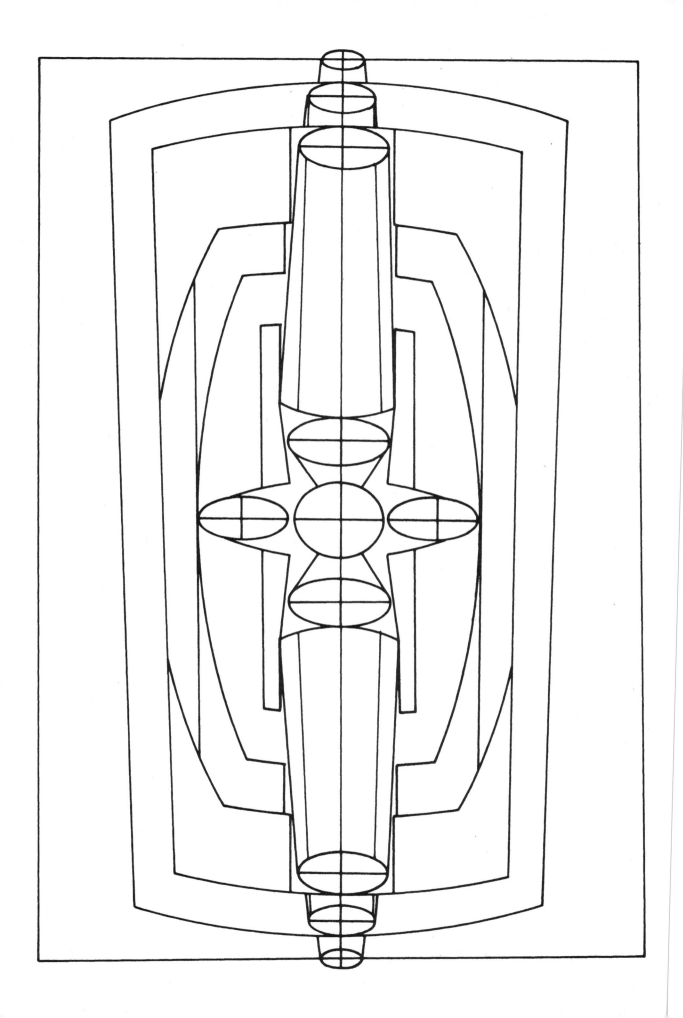

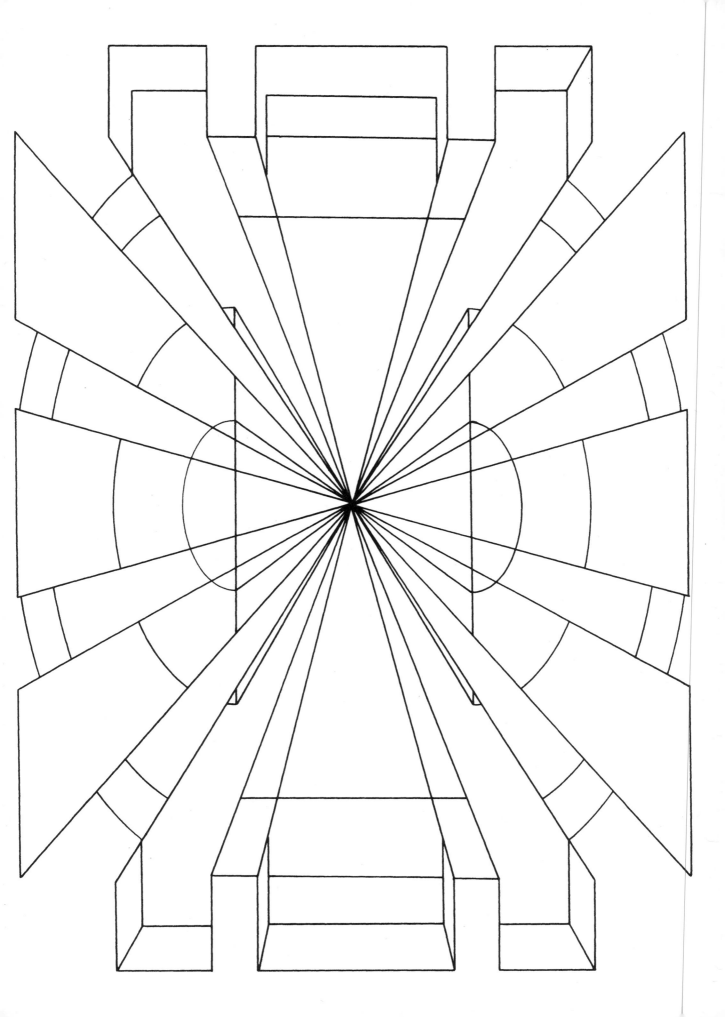

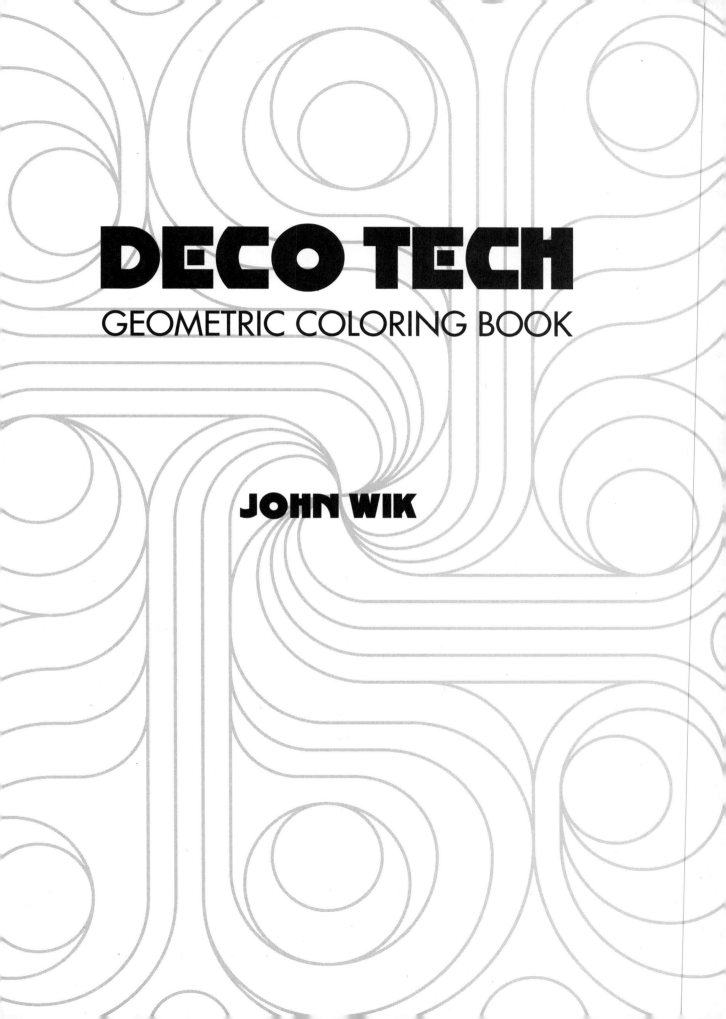